The Animal

Kingdom

Written by Tess Schembri

Series Consultant: Linda Hoyt

WorldWise
Content-based Learning

Contents

Chapter 1

Living things

What is a living thing?

Non-living rock

What do an elephant and a mushroom have in common? They are both living things and share the characteristics of living things.

Non-living fire

Living things need food to give them energy. Animals take in food by eating plants or other animals. Plants produce their own food. Bacteria and fungi survive by feeding on other living things. Protists (algae) eat tiny living things.

Every living thing that we know about has been named so that it can be easily identified. Animals, plants, fungi, **protists (algae)** and **bacteria** all belong to the living world.

Living elephants

All living things grow and change. Some grow quickly, others grow very slowly.

Living things reproduce in many different ways. Most animals and plants need a male and a female part to reproduce.

Living things respond when their environment changes. Most animals move around to find food and shelter. Plants cannot move, but they have many amazing ways of responding to their environment.

The five kingdoms

Living things have been divided into five main groups that are often called the five kingdoms. The five different kingdoms are explained below.

Kingdom Animalia (Animals)

What are they made from?
Many large complicated cells.

What do they feed on?
Other living things.

How many are there?
More than one million species.

Examples: Insects, fish, humans and birds.

Kingdom Plantae (Plants)

What are they made from?
Large complicated cells.

What do they feed on?
Make their own food from sunlight.

How many are there?
About 350,000 species.

Examples: Mosses, ferns, trees and flowering plants.

Kingdom Fungi (Fungi)

What are they made from?
Many simple cells.

What do they feed on?
Other living things.

How many are there?
More than 100,000 species.

Examples: Mushrooms, moulds and yeasts.

Kingdom Protista (Protists)

What are they made from?
One tiny, complicated cell.

What do they feed on?
Tiny living things.

How many are there?
More than 100,000 species.

Examples: Green, golden, brown and red algae.

Kingdom Monera (Bacteria)

What are they made from?
One tiny, simple cell.

What do they feed on?
Other living things.

How many are there?
More than 10,000 species.

Examples: Tetanus and pneumonia.

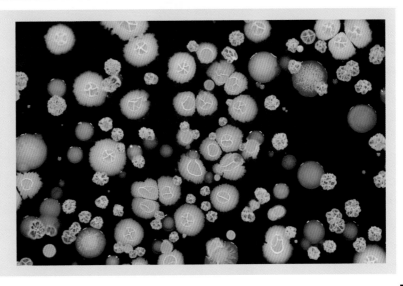

Looking at animals

Animals feed

Animals are consumers. They take in food by eating plants or other animals. This gives animals energy, which they need to move, to grow and to produce **offspring**.

Animals grow

Animals grow and change as they get older. Their lifetimes can range from a few days to more than 100 years. Usually animals look different as adults compared to when they were very young.

Find out more

An elephant needs to eat 140–180 kilograms of food each day. What are some of the things elephants eat? Where do elephants find their food?

Animals reproduce

Most animals need a male and a female to make a new animal like them. Usually the female gives birth or lays the eggs. Sometimes the male will **fertilise** the eggs after they are laid.

Animals respond

Animals respond to different things. If animals sense danger, they move away. If there is no food to eat, they go to find food. They seek shelter if they are too cold or too hot. Most animals have particular characteristics that help them survive in their natural habitat.

How long do animals live?	
Animal	Lifetime
Box turtle	100 years
Polar bear	20 years
Gorilla	20 years
Lobster	15 years
Dog	12 years
Leopard	12 years
Giraffe	10 years
Squirrel	10 years
Guinea pig	4 years
Opossum	1 year
Spring azure butterfly	4 days

Find out more

Does the mother or father seahorse hatch the live baby seahorses?

Fish
Most fish lay eggs, but some give birth to live young.

Birds
All birds lay eggs.

Mammals
Most mammals give birth to live young. A few mammals lay eggs.

Insects
Most insects lay eggs.

Reptiles
Most reptiles lay eggs.

Chapter 2

Classification

Carl Linnaeus,
1707–1778

A name for all things

Living things are named and grouped so they are easy to **identify** and study. This is called classification. **Scientists** classify living things according to their similarities and differences. They examine the **characteristics** of each thing and then decide which group it should belong to.

Carl Linnaeus was a scientist who created a system of naming and classifying living things. He gave each living thing two names. One name was for the larger group that the living thing belonged to, and the other name was for the thing itself.

Carl Linnaeus gave the name *Panthera* to all large roaring cats. Tigers, lions and jaguars are all large roaring cats. Their pictures (right) are labelled with their scientific names.

Tiger
Panthera tigris

Lion
Panthera leo

Jaguar
Panthera onca

Find out more

Which language did Carl Linnaeus choose to use when classifying animals and plants? Why did he make this choice?

The Canada goose

The Latin names given to animals sometimes change. The Aleutian Canada goose has had ten different names because scientists can't decide if it is a subspecies of Canada goose or if it is a goose **species** of its own.

The panda

As more information is learned about a species, its classification may change. Scientists have classified the red panda and the giant panda into different species because of the way they look. At one time, the red panda was in the raccoon family and the giant panda was in the bear family even though they are both known as pandas.

11

The animal kingdom

All animals belong to the animal kingdom. There are more than one million species of animals in the animal kingdom.

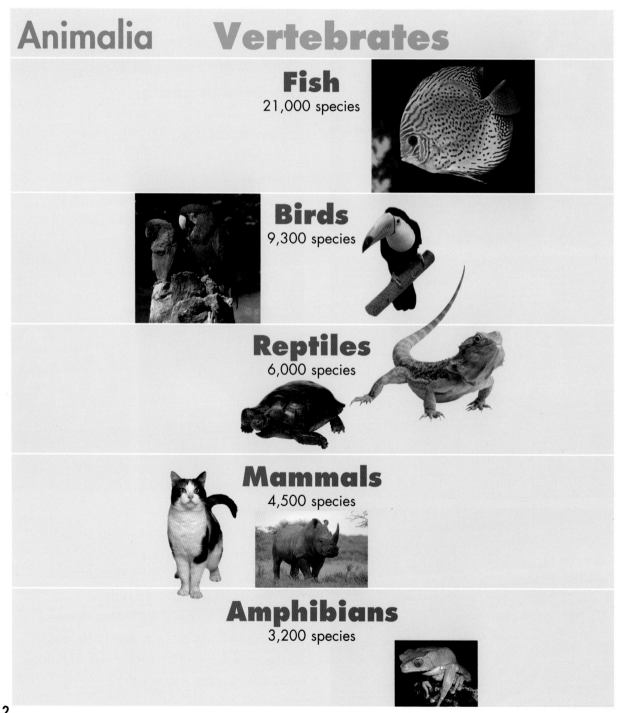

Animalia   Vertebrates

Fish
21,000 species

Birds
9,300 species

Reptiles
6,000 species

Mammals
4,500 species

Amphibians
3,200 species

Scientists have divided the animal kingdom into two groups: vertebrates (animals with backbones) and invertebrates (animals without backbones).

Animalia Invertebrates

Insects
one million species

Molluscs
50,000 species

Crustaceans
42,000 species

Arachnids
30,000 species

Flatworms
25,000 species

Roundworms
10,000 species

Stinging animals
9,000 species

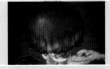

Segmented worms
8,800 species

Echinoderms
5,000 species

Sponges
5,000 species

Vertebrates

Vertebrates are animals that have a spine made of bones called vertebrae. They can be very different from each other, but all vertebrates have a spine. Some can fly, some can swim and some can walk. They are divided into five main groups: fish, birds, reptiles, mammals and amphibians.

Find out more

Not all animal skeletons are made from bone. Do you know what shark skeletons are made from?

Facts about vertebrates

- Vertebrates have billions of body cells.
- Vertebrates have matching right and left sides of the body.
- Vertebrates never have more than two pairs of limbs.

Characteristics and types of vertebrates

Fish

Bodies: Covered with scales
Habitat: Live in water
Life cycle: Most hatch from eggs
Examples: Bony fish, sharks, rays, chimeras

Birds

Bodies: Usually covered with feathers
Habitat: Live on land or on water
Life cycle: Hatch from eggs
Examples: Parrots, raptors, waders, seed eaters

Reptiles

Bodies: Usually covered with scales
Habitat: Most live on land, some live in water
Life cycle: Most hatch from eggs
Examples: Alligators, lizards, snakes, turtles

Mammals

Bodies: Covered with skin and some hair
Habitat: Most live on land, some live in water
Life cycle: Most young born alive
Examples: Dolphins, bears, marsupials, rodents

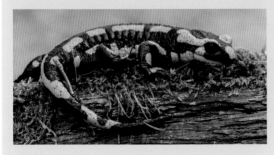

Amphibians

Bodies: Usually covered with skin
Habitat: Live in water and on land
Life cycle: Most hatch from eggs
Examples: Frogs, toads, salamanders

Invertebrates

An invertebrate is an animal that does not have a backbone. Some invertebrates have a soft body, others have a hard outer skeleton. Most of the animals on Earth are invertebrates. Invertebrates are animals such as beetles, spiders, worms, sea urchins, shrimps, snails and flies.

Characteristics and types of invertebrates

Insects
Bodies: Three main body parts – head, thorax, and **abdomen**. Bodies covered with a hard external skeleton.
Habitat: In water and on land
Examples: Bees, ants, termites, butterflies, cockroaches, beetles, fireflies, mosquitoes

Molluscs
Bodies: Soft body with a hard outer shell
Habitat: In water and some on land
Examples: Clams, oysters, mussels, snails

Crustaceans – shellfish
Bodies: Soft body with a hard outer shell
Habitat: In water and some on land
Examples: Crabs, crayfish, shrimp

Arachnids – spiders
Bodies: Bodies have three main parts
Habitat: On land (not in the Antarctic) and some in water (not in oceans)
Examples: Spiders, ticks, mites, scorpions

Flatworms – worms
Bodies: Smooth, soft body covered with skin
Habitat: In water or inside other animals
Examples: Flatworms, flukes, tapeworms

Design your own animal

If you had to design a new animal, would it be a vertebrate or an invertebrate?
Where would it live?
What would it feed on?
What body parts would it have?

Roundworms – worms

Bodies: Soft, round, threadlike body
Habitat: In soil, water, dead plants, or dead animals
Examples: Hookworms and pinworms

Stinging animals

Bodies: Cylinder-, bell-, or umbrella-shaped body
Habitat: In seawater or in **freshwater**
Examples: Sea jellies, sea anemone, coral

Segmented worms

Bodies: Soft body divided into ringlike sections
Habitat: In water and on land
Examples: Earthworms, leeches

Echinoderms

Bodies: A skeleton covered with spiny skin
Habitat: In the sea
Examples: Sea stars, sand dollars, sea cucumbers

Sponges

Bodies: A skeleton covered with soft material
Habitat: Salt water and freshwater
Examples: Sponges

Chapter 3 How are animals different?

Names can be tricky!

Fish, jellyfish and starfish all have the word fish in their common name, but they are not all fish. **Scientists** call jellyfish sea jellies because they are not fish. Scientists call starfish sea stars because they are not fish. The names we use every day do not always tell you what you need to know.

Fish

Group: Vertebrates – fish

Body covering: Scales

Feeding: Fish eat through their mouths. They have teeth or hard plates that they use to capture and eat their food.

Moving: Swim using their fins and tails. Many fish are fast swimmers.

Life cycle: Most fish lay eggs. Some fish keep the eggs inside their bodies until they hatch, and others have live young. Young fish look like their parents.

Sea jellies (jellyfish)

Group: Invertebrates – stinging animals

Body covering: Skin

Feeding: Sea jellies use their stinging tentacles to kill or **paralyse** their prey. They have a large mouth underneath their body.

Moving: Slowly open and close their bell-shaped bodies to drift or swim through the water

Life cycle: Sea jellies release eggs and sperm into the ocean. The eggs grow into **larvae** and then into **polyps**. The polyps divide to make new polyps, and these grow into sea jellies.

Sea star (starfish)

Group: Invertebrates – echinoderms

Body covering: Spines

Feeding: Sea stars use the suction tubes on their feet to open shellfish. They eat by putting their stomach out through their mouth and into the shellfish's shell.

Moving: Walk by pushing water through their tube feet

Life cycle: Sea stars release eggs and sperm into the ocean. The eggs grow into larvae and drift around until they change into sea stars.

Looks can be deceiving!

Sometimes animals look the same. Dolphins and sharks have similar-shaped bodies, they both live in the sea and are about the same size. Are dolphins and sharks the same? Compare these diagrams to find out.

| bone skeleton | smooth skin | lungs | teeth |

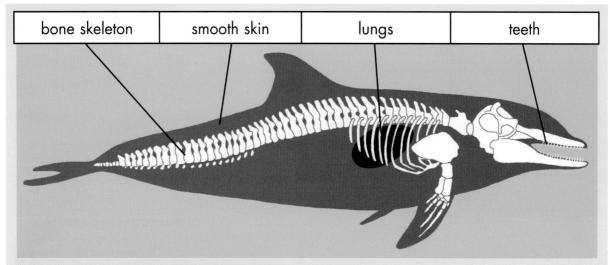

Dolphins

Group: Mammal – vertebrate

Body parts: A skeleton made of bone. They have smooth skin that feels like rubber. Dolphins breathe air through their lungs.

Teeth: Dolphins have a single row of cone-shaped teeth in both jaws. They use their teeth to hold and puncture their prey. Dolphins swallow their food whole or in large chunks.

Food: Dolphins eat fish, squid and other sea creatures.

Blood temperature: Always stays the same

Life cycle: Dolphins are born alive and are looked after by their mother. They feed on her milk until they can feed themselves.

| teeth | gills | sharp scales | cartilage skeleton |

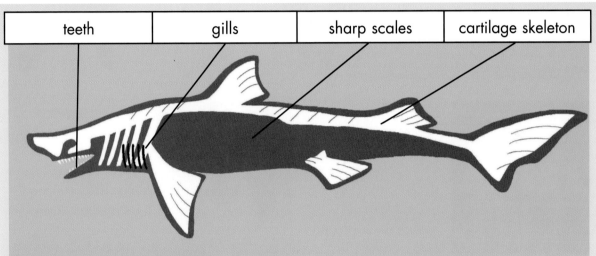

Shark

Group: Fish – vertebrate

Body parts: A skeleton made of **cartilage**. They have sharp scales that are like tiny teeth, and their bodies feel like sandpaper. Sharks breathe in water using gills.

Teeth: Some sharks have many rows of razor-sharp teeth in both jaws. They use their teeth to tear their prey into bite-size pieces and swallow it without chewing.

Food: Sharks eat fish, squid and other sea creatures.

Blood temperature: Changes with water temperature

Life cycle: Some sharks develop from eggs inside their mother and are born alive. Some sharks lay eggs. Young sharks feed themselves.

Same but different

All dogs belong to the same group. They are all mammals.
Over time people have bred dogs from wolves. They have been
bred to do different things so they have specific **characteristics**.

Non-sporting dogs
Non-sporting dogs include different
types of dogs that have been
bred in different ways. They
include bulldogs, dalmatians
and standard poodles.

Hounds
Hounds are dogs that
run fast and have
an excellent sense of
smell. Some hounds
are the Afghan
hound, the foxhound
and bloodhound.

Herding dogs
Herding dogs
can run fast over
long distances.
Border collies and
Australian cattle
dogs are herding
dogs.

Working dogs
Working dogs can
pull sleds, guard
property and rescue
people. They are
dogs such as the
Siberian husky,
Labrador and
beagle.

Sporting dogs
Sporting dogs can
run fast and need
lots of exercise.
Spaniels and
retrievers are
sporting dogs.

Terriers
Terriers have a keen
sense of smell. They
like to dig in the
ground to find foxes,
rabbits or rats.
Jack Russells and
Airedales are terriers.

Toy dogs
Toy dogs are the
smallest breeds of
dogs. They are
dogs such as the
Pekingese and the
chihuahua.

Glossary

abdomen the part of the body that encloses the stomach, pelvis, ribs and intestine

algae a tiny plant

bacteria tiny organisms that are present everywhere; some bacteria cause disease in humans, but many others are useful to us

cartilage the tough elastic material that makes up a shark's skeletal system

cells organisms that make living things grow

characteristics what makes things similar or different

fertilise to make an egg produce a live animal

freshwater water that is not salty

identify to know what group something belongs to

larvae newly hatched insects in wormlike form

offspring the animal that is born or hatched from a parent

paralyse to make an animal unable to move

polyps the early stages of a sea jelly's life

protist a plant with only one cell

scientists people who study living and non-living things

species a biological grouping of closely related living things

Index